Disney
Songs for vibraphone

Arranged by Patrick Roulet

ISBN 978-1-5400-2214-1

Characters and Artwork © Disney
Disney/Pixar elements © Disney/Pixar

The following songs are the property of:

Bourne Co.
Music Publishers
www.bournemusic.com

Some Day My Prince Will Come
When You Wish Upon A Star

Visit Hal Leonard Online at
www.halleonard.com

Contact us:
Hal Leonard
7777 West Bluemound Road
Milwaukee, WI 53213
Email: info@halleonard.com

In Europe, contact:
Hal Leonard Europe Limited
42 Wigmore Street
Marylebone, London, W1U 2RN
Email: info@halleonardeurope.com

In Australia, contact:
Hal Leonard Australia Pty. Ltd.
4 Lentara Court
Cheltenham, Victoria, 3192 Australia
Email: info@halleonard.com.au

To Charlotte and Celia

Colors of the Wind
from POCAHONTAS

Music by Alan Menken
Lyrics by Stephen Schwartz

× = Mallet dampen

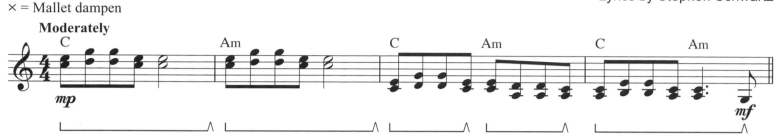

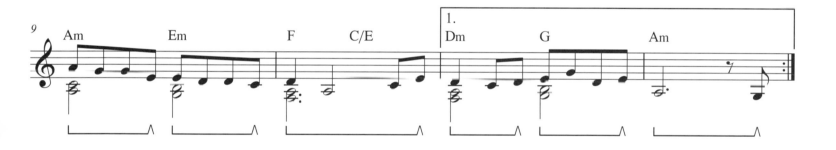

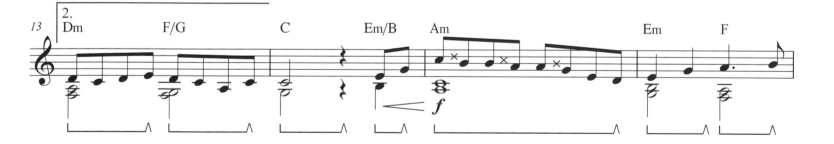

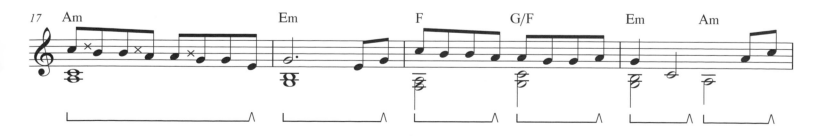

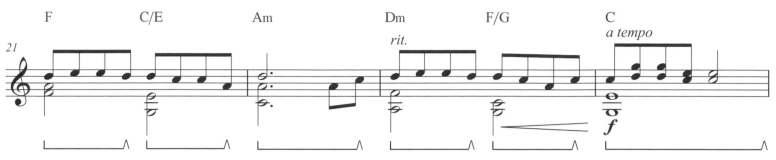

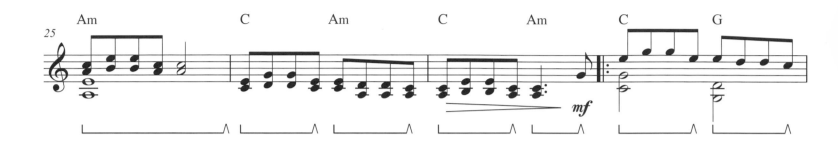

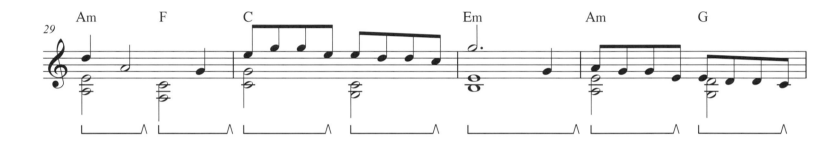

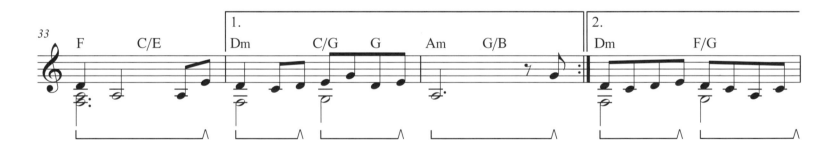

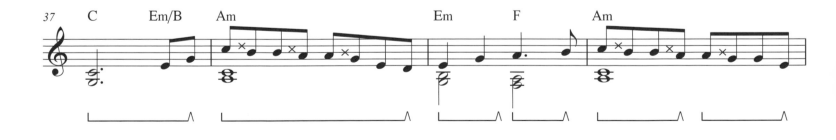

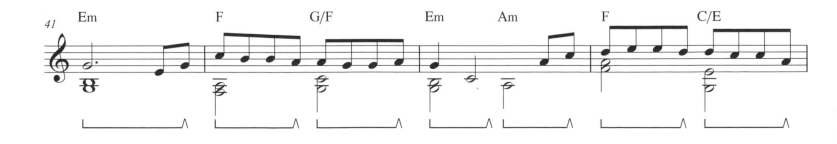

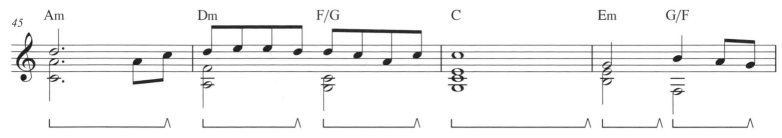

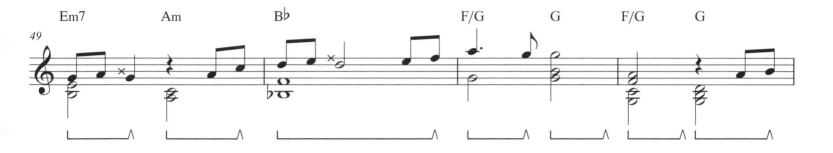

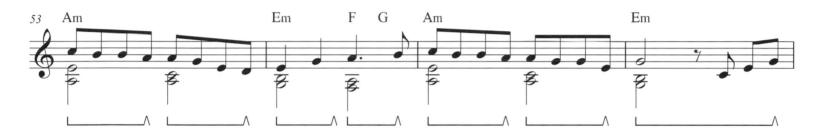

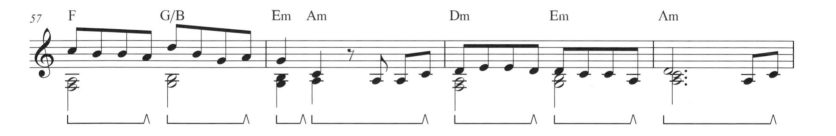

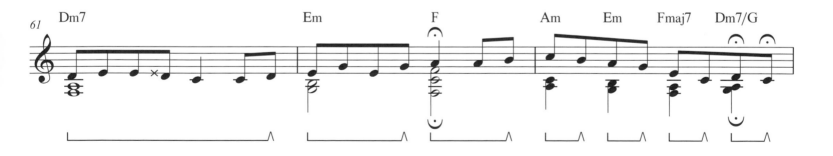

The Bare Necessities
from THE JUNGLE BOOK

Words and Music by
Terry Gilkyson

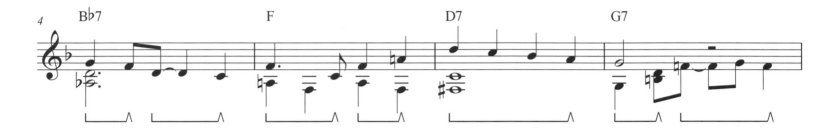

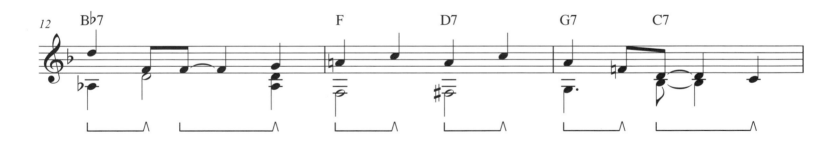

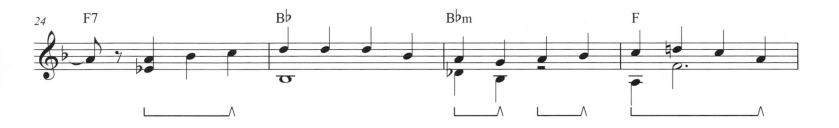

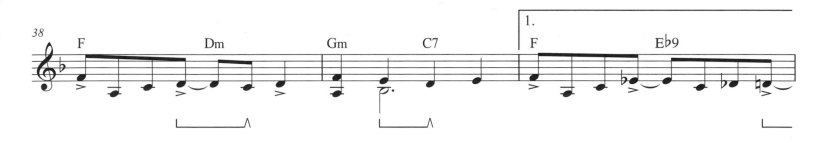

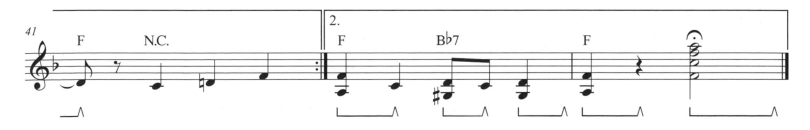

Beauty and the Beast

from BEAUTY AND THE BEAST

Music by Alan Menken
Lyrics by Howard Ashman

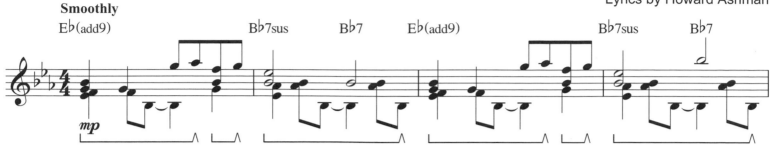

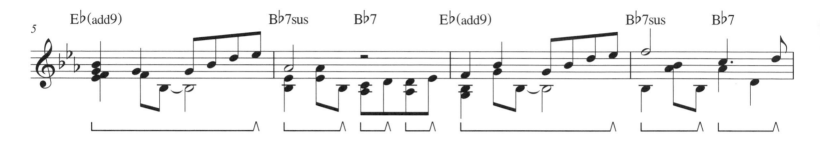

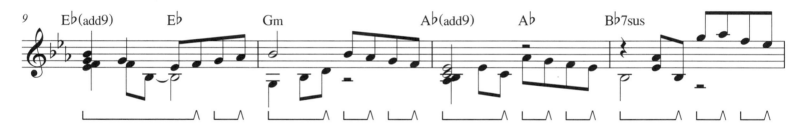

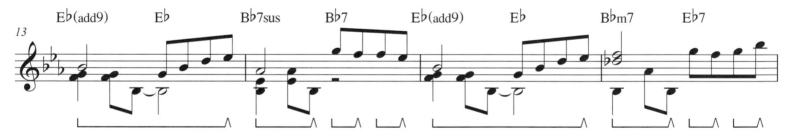

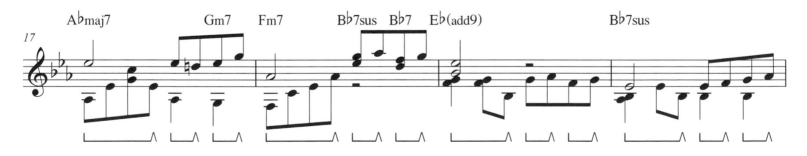

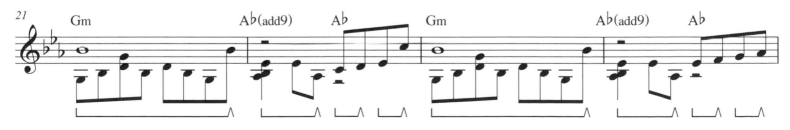

Can You Feel the Love Tonight

from THE LION KING

Music by Elton John
Lyrics by Tim Rice

× = Mallet dampen

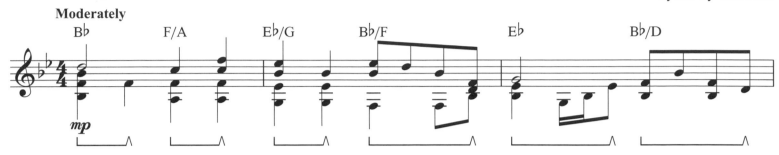

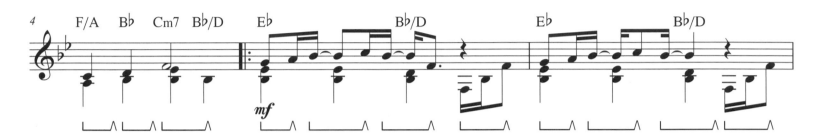

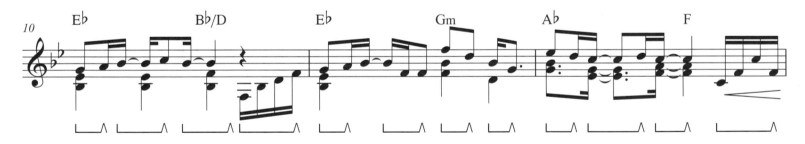

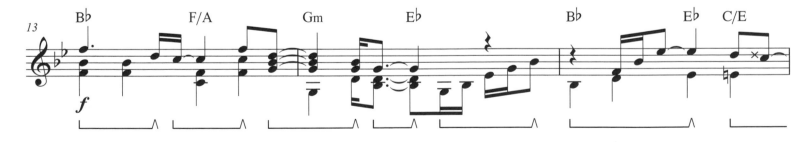

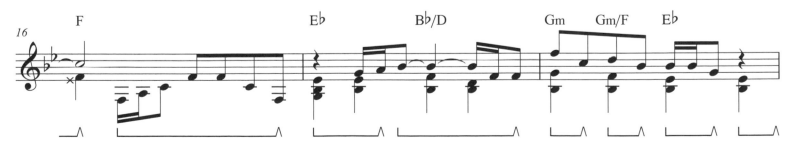

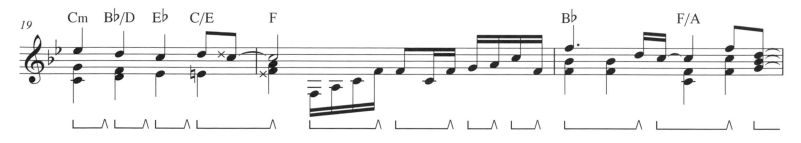

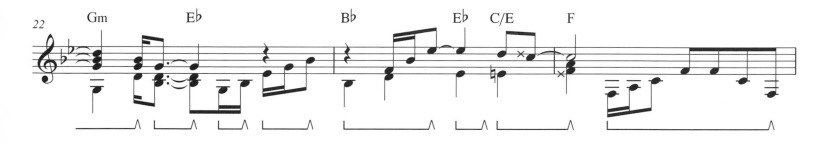

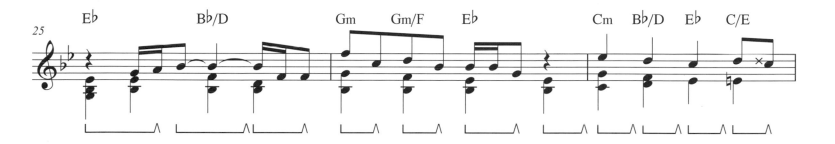

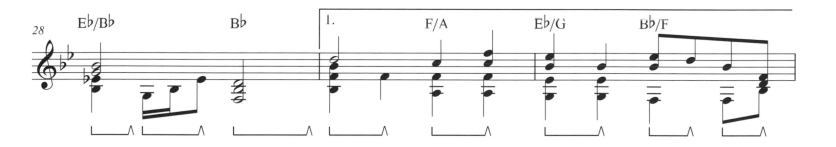

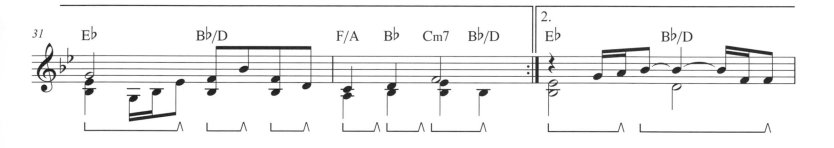

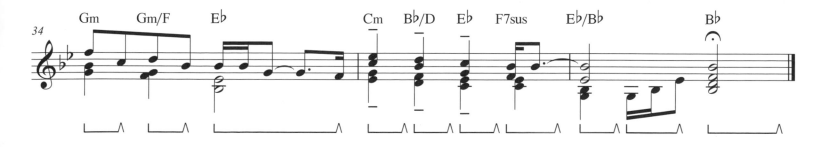

Cruella De Vil
from 101 DALMATIANS

Words and Music by
Mel Leven

Slow Blues

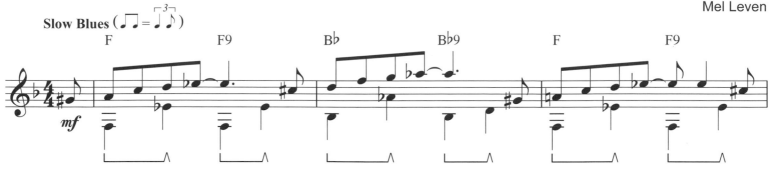

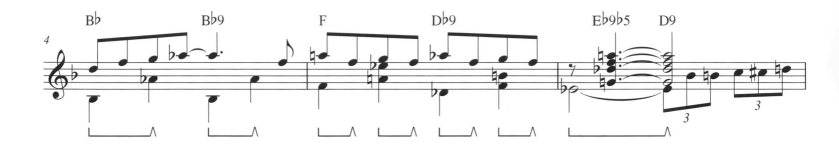

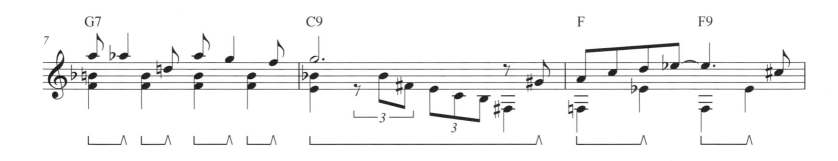

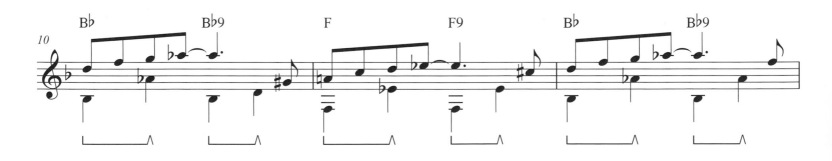

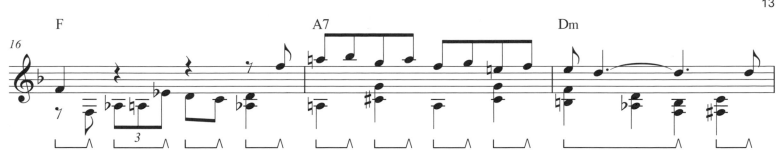

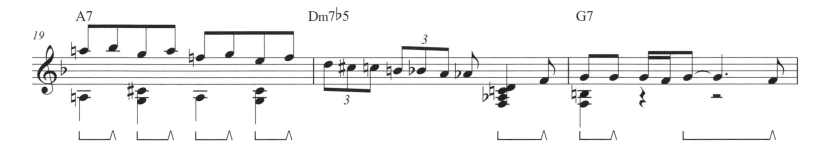

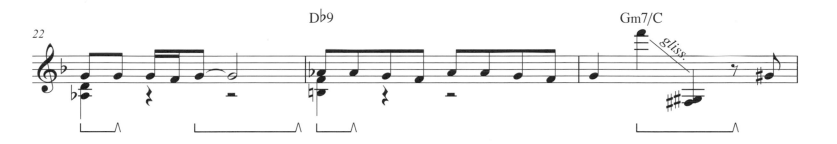

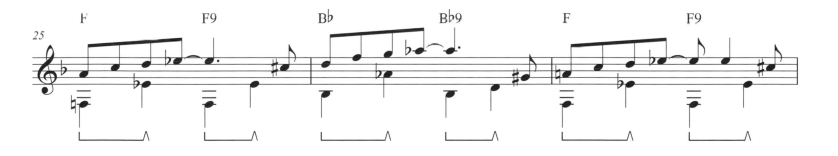

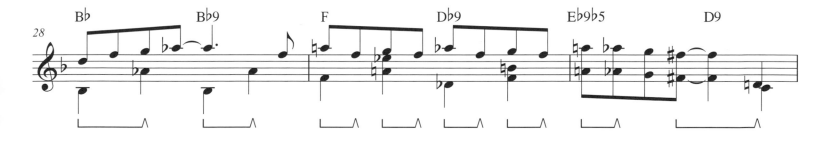

Do You Want to Build a Snowman?

from FROZEN

× = Mallet dampen
○ = Play harmonic with left hand mallet on node

Music and Lyrics by Kristen Anderson-Lopez
and Robert Lopez

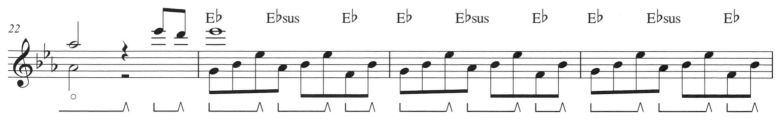

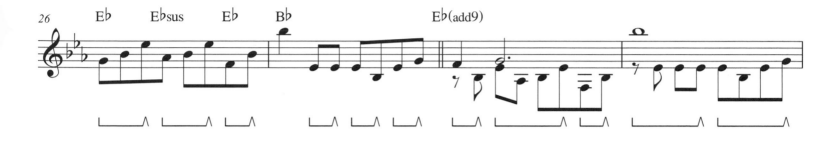

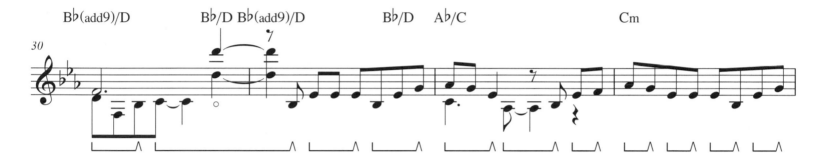

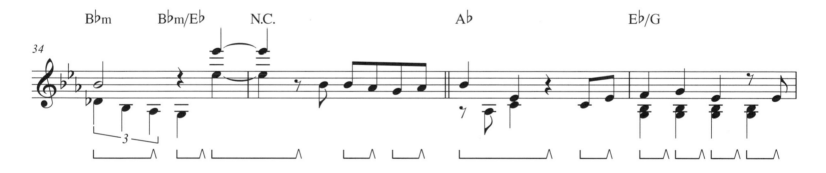

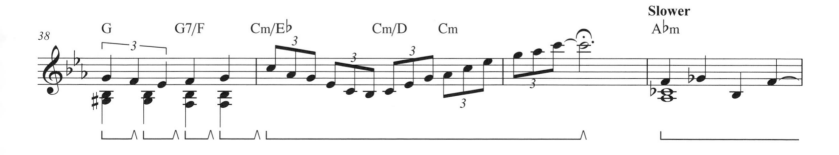

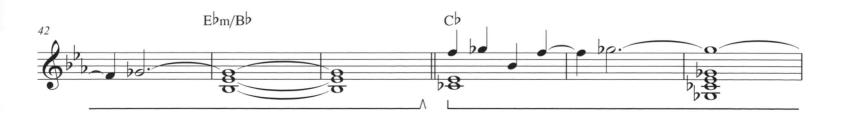

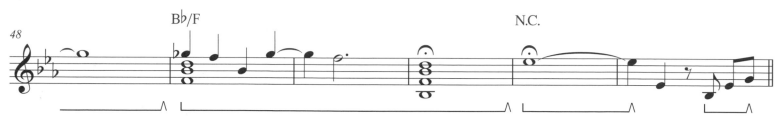

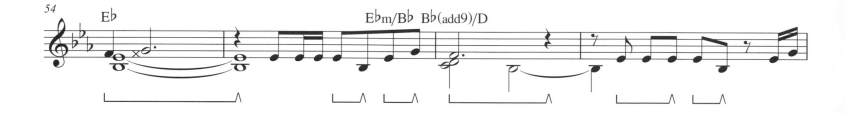

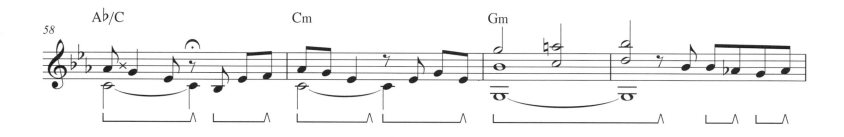

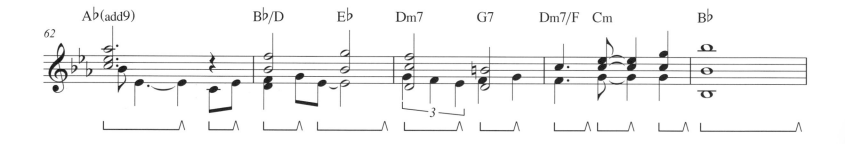

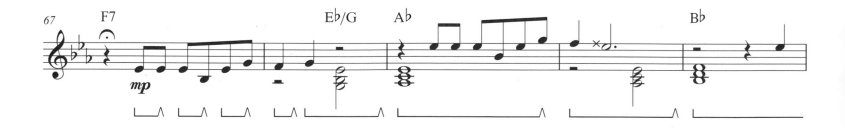

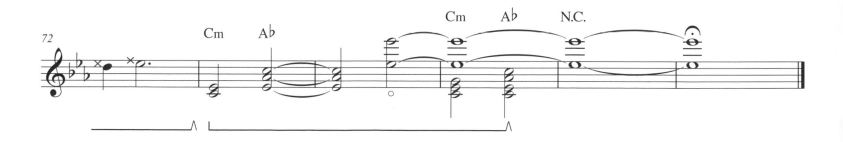

Some Day My Prince Will Come

from SNOW WHITE AND THE SEVEN DWARFS

Words by Larry Morey
Music by Frank Churchill

Feed the Birds
(Tuppence a Bag)
from MARY POPPINS

Words and Music by Richard M. Sherman
and Robert B. Sherman

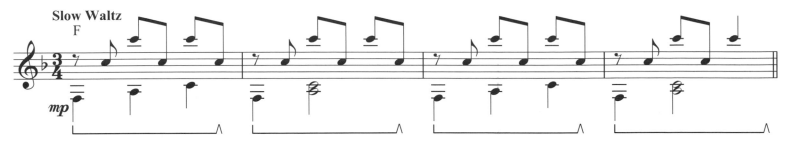

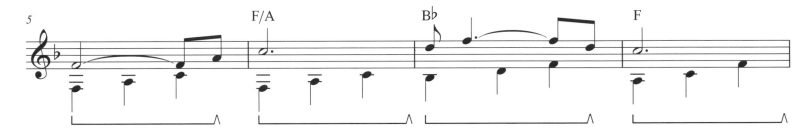

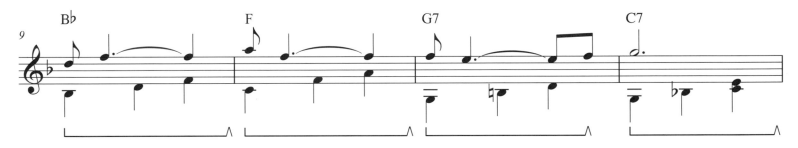

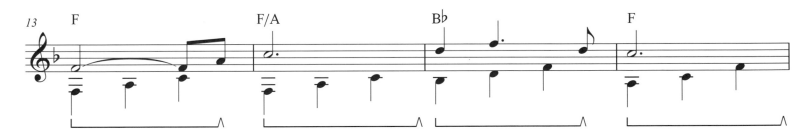

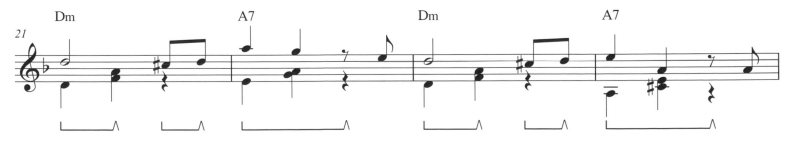

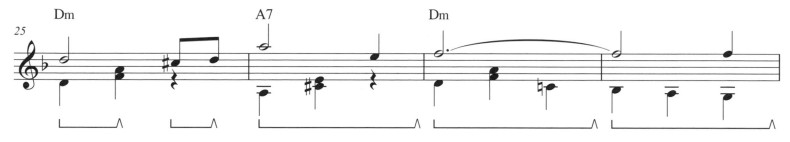

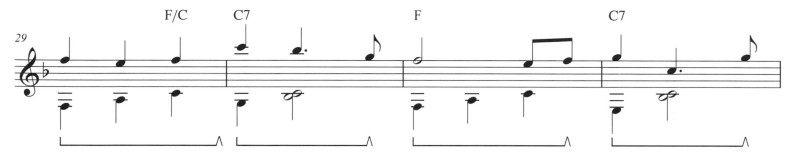

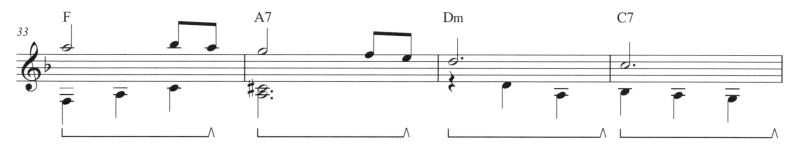

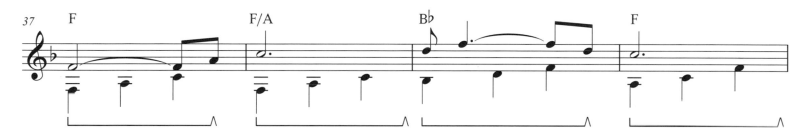

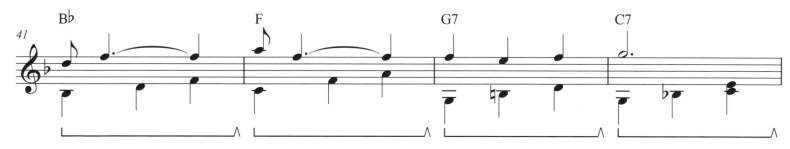

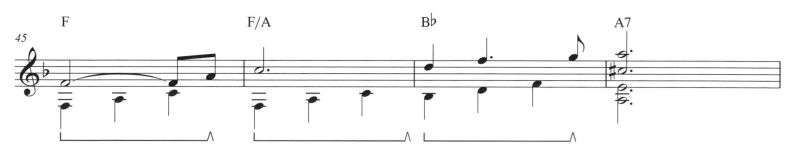

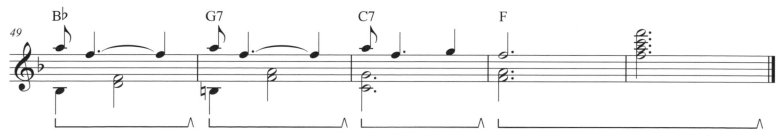

He's a Pirate
from PIRATES OF THE CARIBBEAN: THE CURSE OF THE BLACK PEARL

Written by Hans Zimmer,
Klaus Badelt and Geoff Zanelli

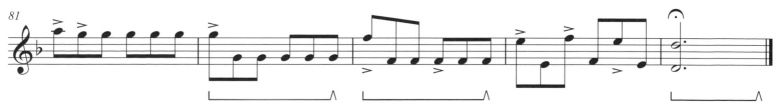

Kiss the Girl
from THE LITTLE MERMAID

Music by Alan Menken
Lyrics by Howard Ashman

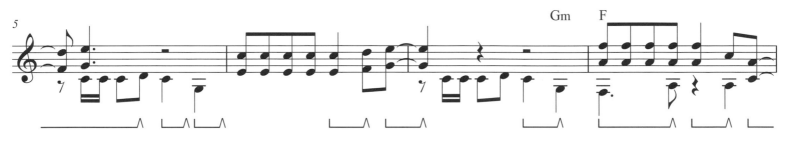

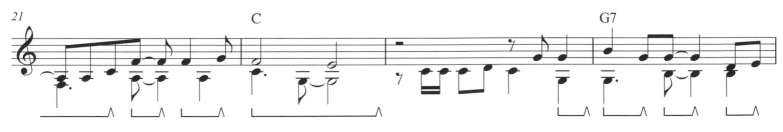

Under the Sea
from THE LITTLE MERMAID

Music by Alan Menken
Lyrics by Howard Ashman

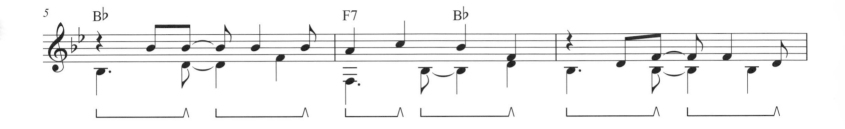

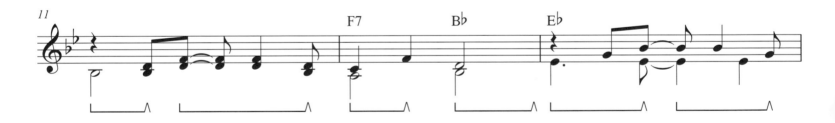

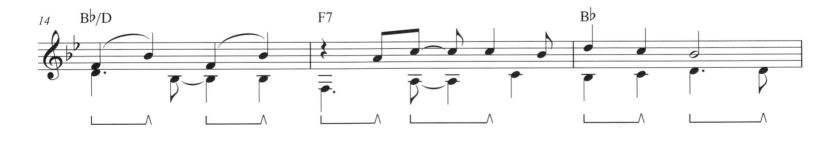

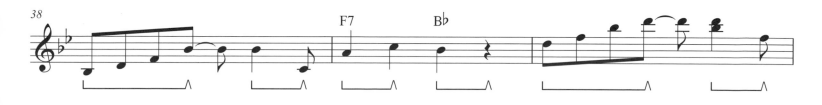

When She Loved Me

from TOY STORY 2

Music and Lyrics by
Randy Newman

× = Mallet dampen

Tenderly

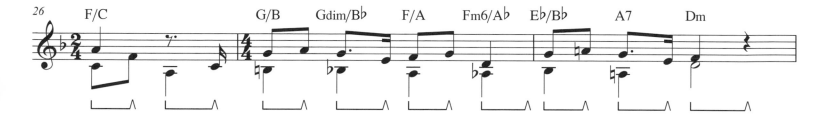

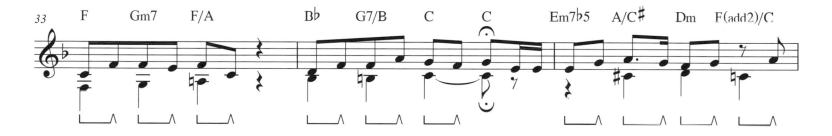

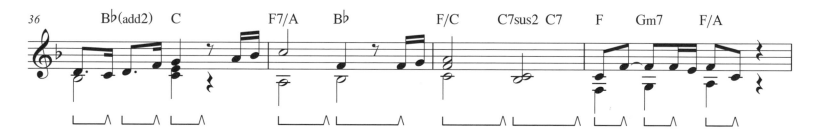

When You Wish Upon A Star
from PINOCCHIO

× = Mallet dampen

Words by Ned Washington
Music by Leigh Harline

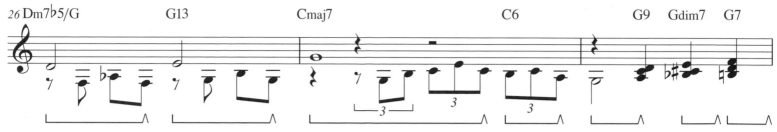

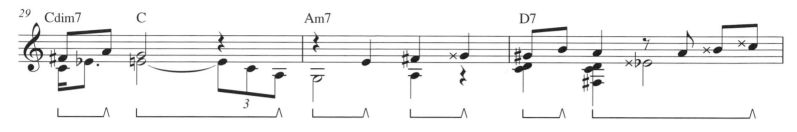

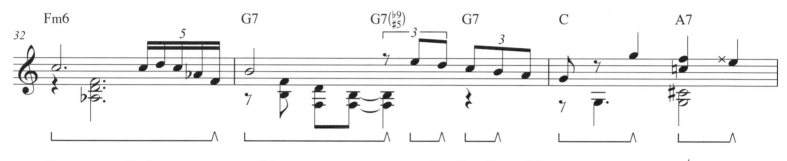

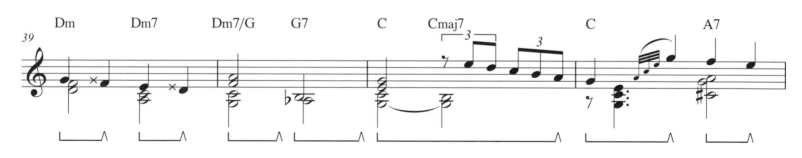

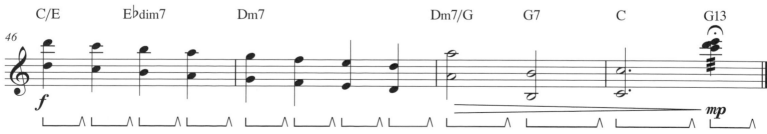

You've Got a Friend in Me
from TOY STORY

Music and Lyrics by
Randy Newman

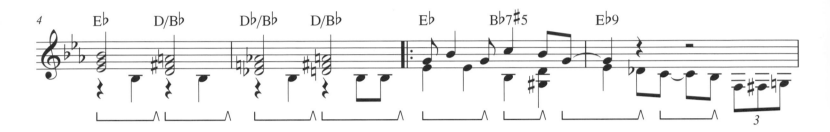

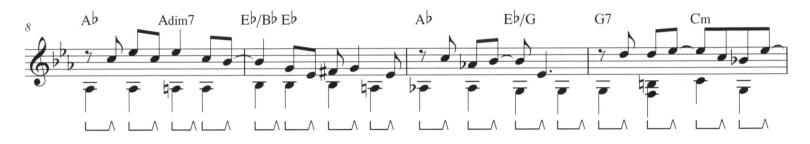

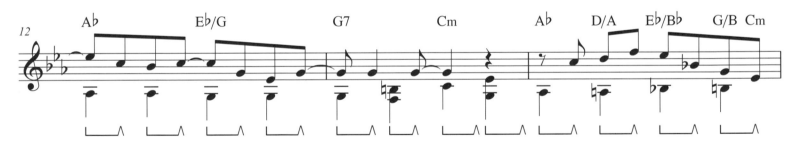

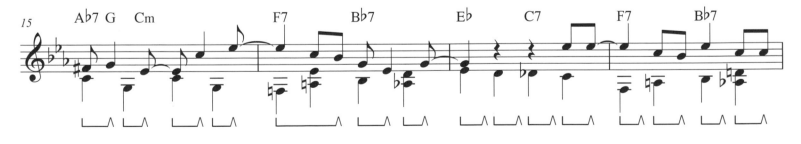

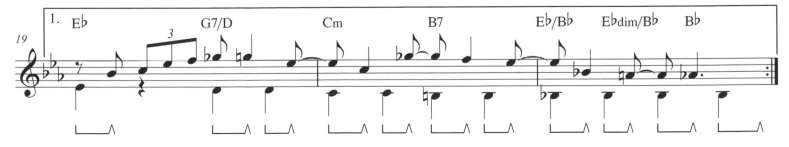

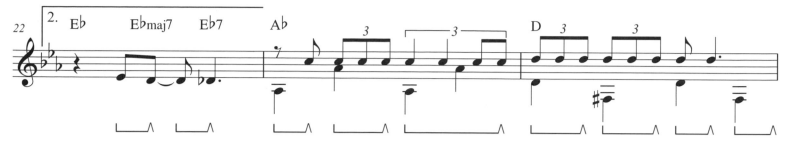

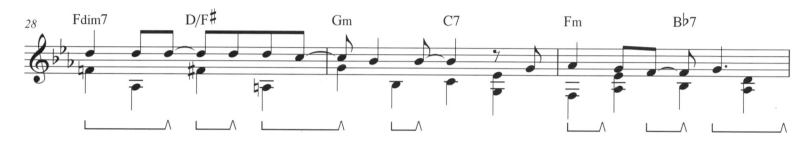

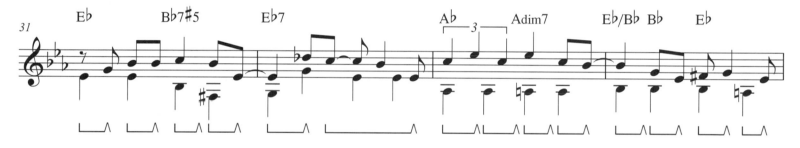

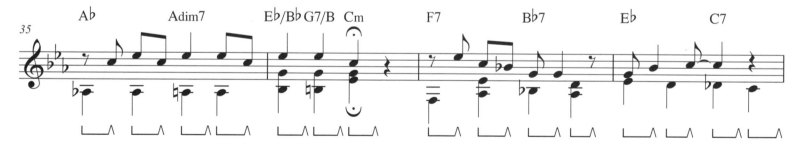

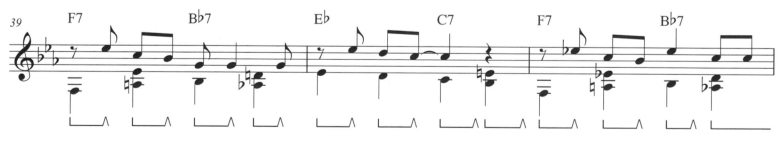

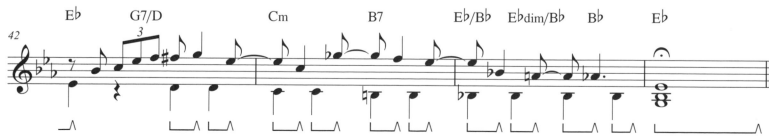

A Whole New World

(Aladdin's Theme)
from ALADDIN

Music by Alan Menken
Lyrics by Tim Rice

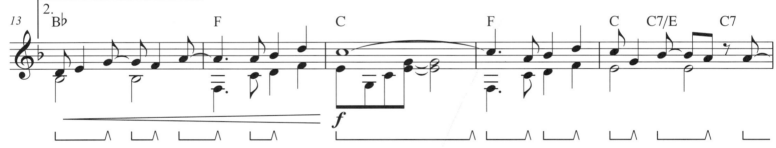

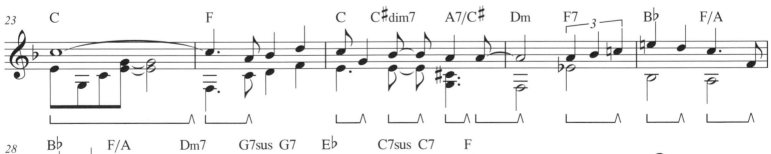